What Good Is a Tail?

Marlene M. Robinson

Illustrated with photographs

DODD, MEAD & COMPANY NEW YORK

Distributed in Canada by
McClelland and Stewart Limited, Toronto
Manufactured in the United States of America
Designed by Mina Greenstein

10 9 8 7 6 5 4 3 2 1

Library of Congress Cataloging in Publication Data

Robinson, Marlene M.
What good is a tail?

Includes index.
Summary: Text and photographs present the appearance and function of the tails of a variety of animals, including the white-tailed deer, rattlesnake, sand tiger shark, and peacock.
1. Tail—Juvenile literature. [1. Tail] I. Title.
QL950.6.R62 1985 596'.049 85-6979
ISBN 0-396-08487-7

PICTURE CREDITS

National Zoological Park, Smithsonian Institution: Office of Exhibits and Graphics, 9 (right), 39, 40; Office of Education, 35, 36; Jessie Cohen, 5, 7, 14. Interior, Sport Fisheries and Wildlife, Office of Audiovisual Services: V. B. Scheffer, 6; Rex Gary Schmidt, 10; Ernest Alfstad, 11; Jim Williams, 29, 30. American Museum of Natural History, Department of Library Services, 8, 13; L. Boltin, 41, 42. Irene Vandermolen, Leonard Rue Enterprises, 9 (left). VIREO, Academy of Natural Sciences: Allan D. Cruickshank, 17, 18, 21 (left), 22, 47 (right); Helen Cruickshank, 12; C. H. Greenewalt, 26; R. Rytter, 19, 20; R. W. VanDevender, 27, 28. Mystic Marinelife Aquarium, Jim Stone, 15, 16, 31, 32, 33, 47 (left). William Beebe, 21 (right), 23, 25. Baltimore Zoo, 24, 34. Francine Schroeder, 37, 38, 43, 44, 45, 46, 47 (center).

TO DOUG

ACKNOWLEDGMENTS

It takes many friends and favors to do a book like this and I am grateful for all assistance. However, a few people deserve extra thanks.

Rob Cardillo and Martine Culbertson of VIREO and Jim Stone of Mystic Marinelife Aquarium have been exceptionally helpful and kind. Judith King, Office of Education, National Zoo; Greg Scholley, Curator of Education, Baltimore Zoo; Craig Koppie of the U.S. Fish & Wildlife Service; Dana Tobin and Dick James of the Schuylkill Valley Nature Center; and budding photographer Jessie Meltzer all deserve special thank yous.

I am most appreciative of the services provided by John DuPont, editor of *The Conservationist*; Janice Hanover of the Australian Embassy; and the Australian Tourist Commission. I am indebted to Jim Naughton and Richard Ben Cramer for contributing memorable, but rejected, titles for a book about tails, and to my husband, Doug, who kept everything in perspective.

What good is a tail?

There are many kinds of animals
with many different tails.
Yet apes and people do not have tails.
Turtles and bears have such small ones,
they can hardly be good for anything.

You can find out how useful animal tails
are by using these clues.
What does the tail look like?
How does it move?

This tail is black and white.
Its shape is big and fluffy.
This forest animal puts its tail to work by lifting it into the air and making it flutter like a flag.
How can that be useful to the animal?

When a **skunk** lifts its
black-and-white tail,
it is a warning.
"Look out!" it says.
Anyone who does not turn and run
may smell like a skunk for many days.

A skunk uses its tail as a warning signal.

Other animals use their tails to send messages, too. Who can tell what these tails are saying?

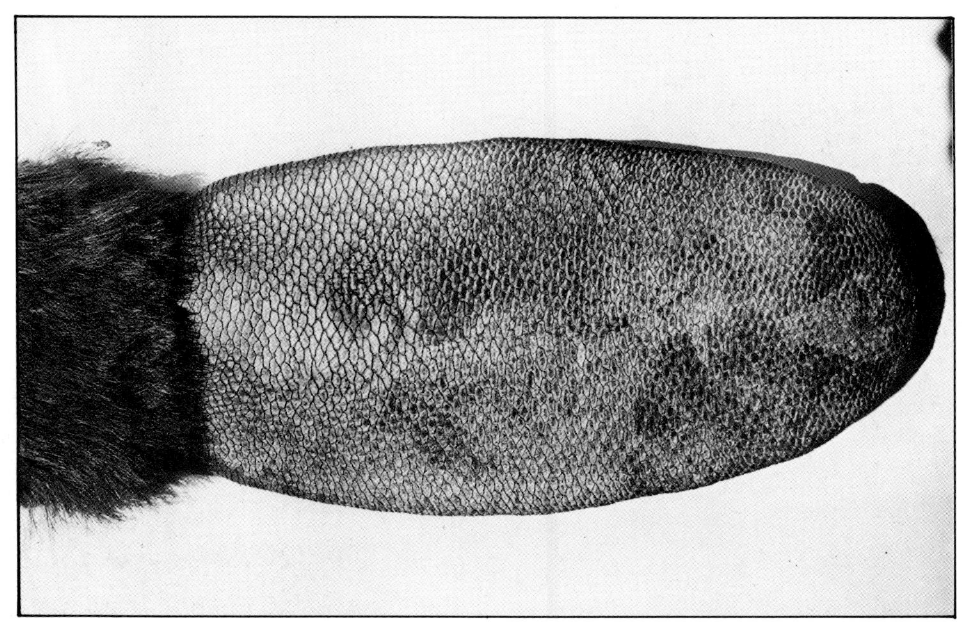

This flat tail moves up and down…

. . . so does this fluffy one.

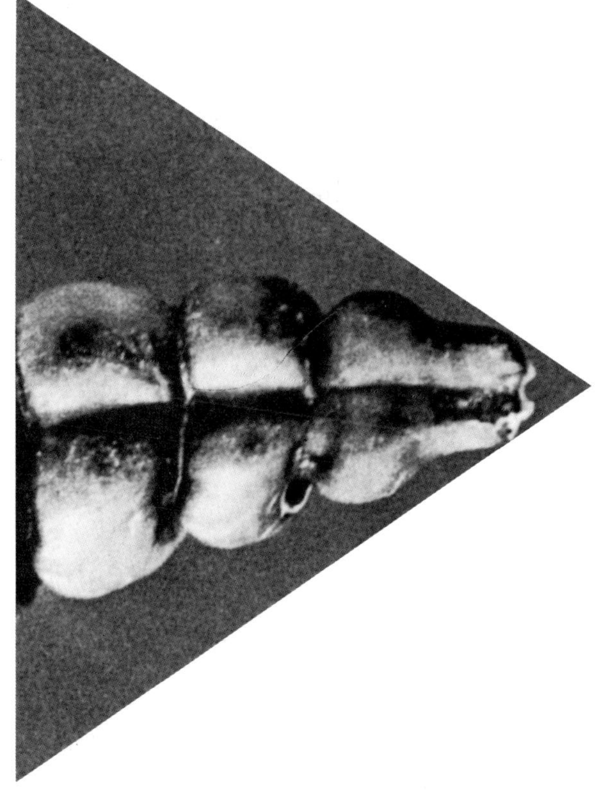

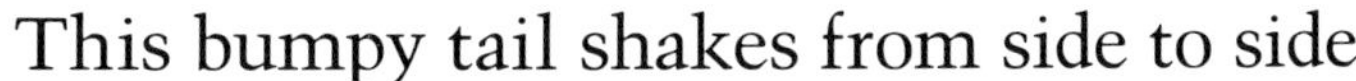

This bumpy tail shakes from side to side.

The **beaver** slaps its flat tail on the surface of the water to warn its family of danger. This loud, sharp sound can be heard across the beaver pond and into the woods.

The beaver also uses its tail when swimming. It helps to steer the animal in the direction it wants to go. When sitting, the beaver uses its tail as a brace.

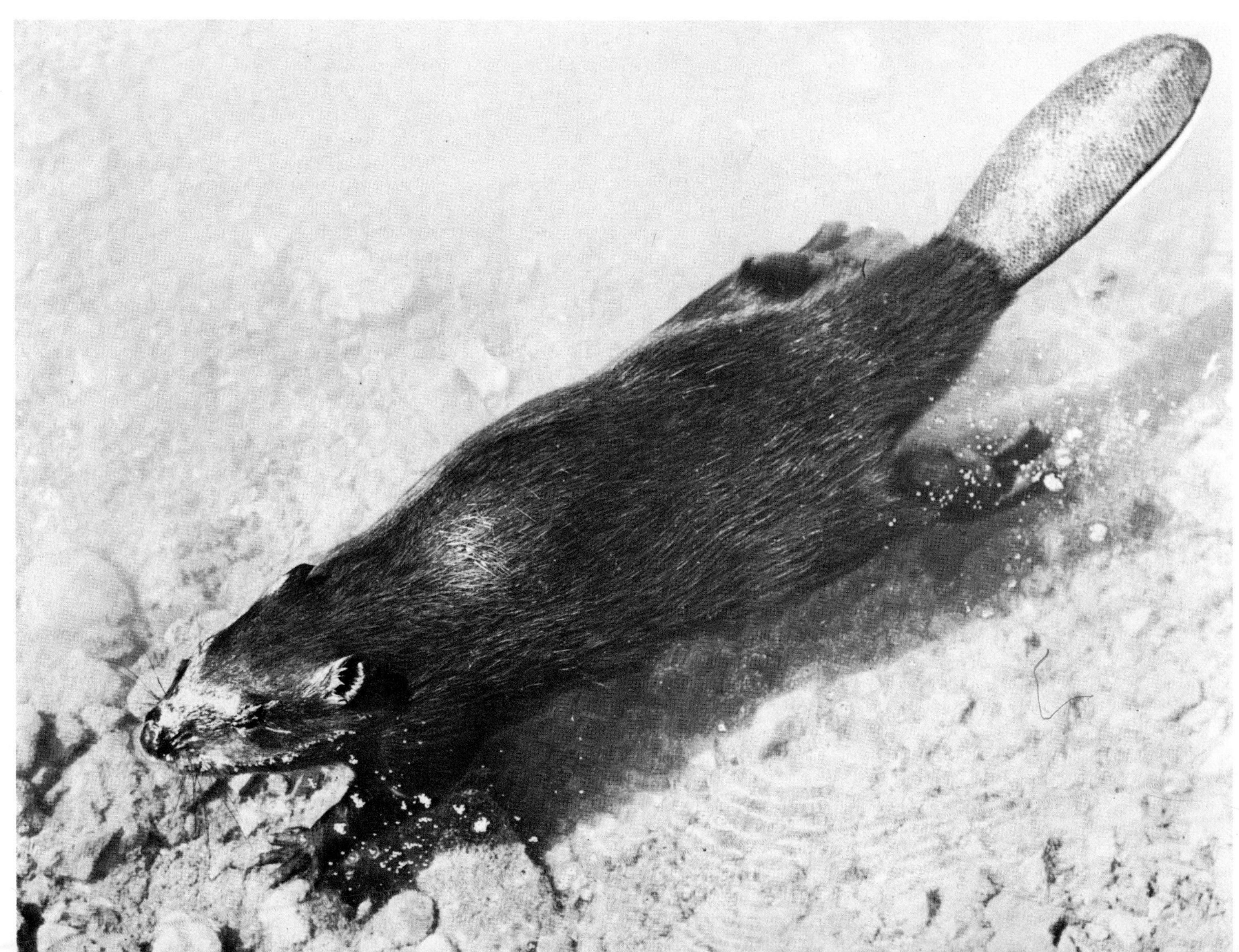

When a **white-tailed deer** senses danger, it raises its tail so the white underside shows. Its white rump also shows.

This is a warning to other deer that there is danger nearby. This white signal is also a guide that young deer can follow into the dark woods.

When the **rattlesnake** shakes its tail,
it is a warning. "Look out! I am ready to strike,"
it says. Anyone who does not move away may receive
a poisonous bite.

Most snakes do not have rattles.
But all snakes have tails.
Where does a tail begin?
Could a snake be all tail?

No, a **snake** has a head, a body, and a tail. They are not always easy to see on a live snake. But the parts are clear on a snake skeleton.

The skull is the snake's head. The backbone and ribs form the body. Where the ribs end, the tail begins. Like most animals, the snake's tail is part of the backbone.

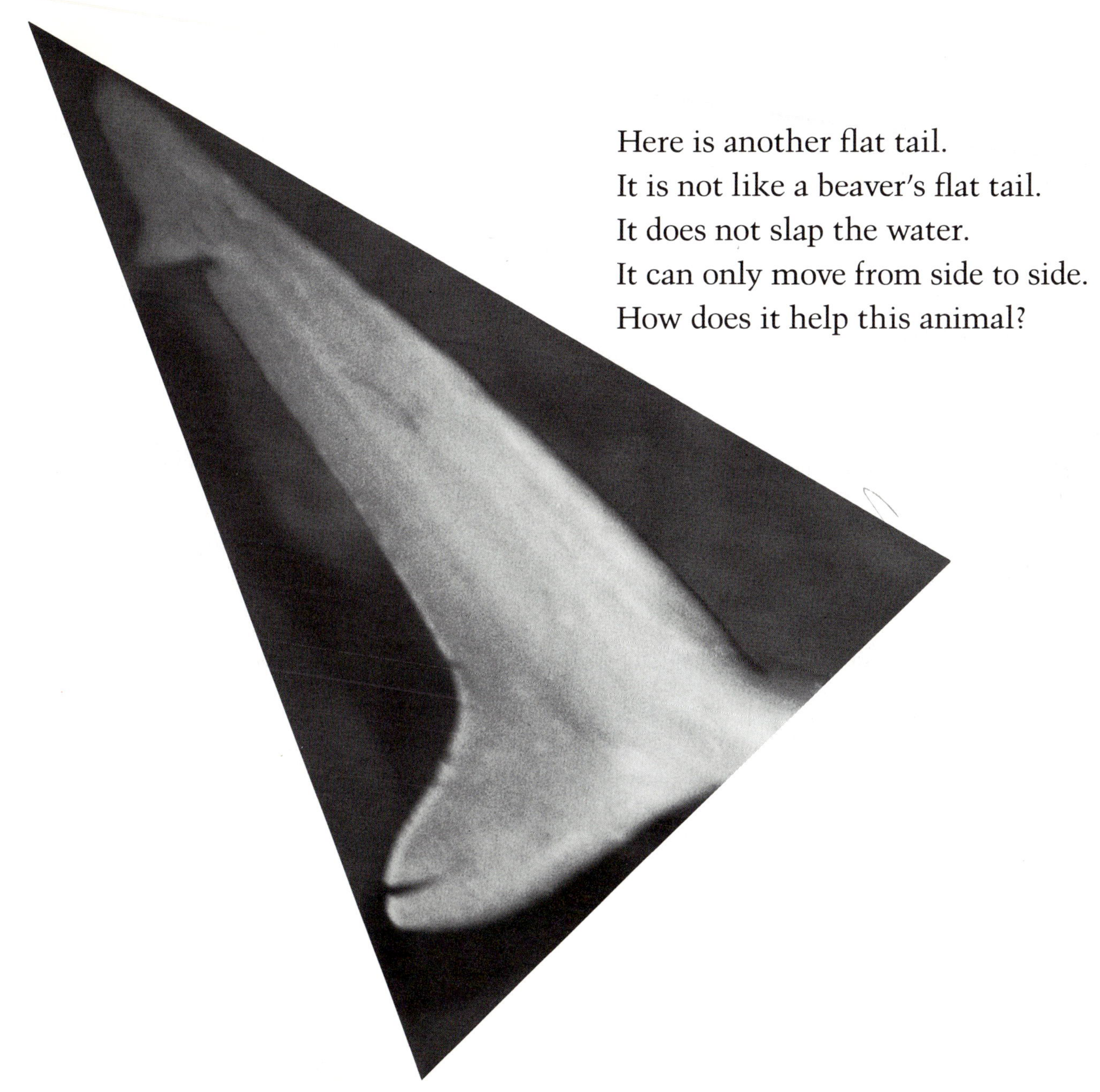

Here is another flat tail.
It is not like a beaver's flat tail.
It does not slap the water.
It can only move from side to side.
How does it help this animal?

This wide, flat tail sends the **sand tiger shark** through the water. The tail swings from side to side with the movement of the animal. This pushes the animal forward.

The long upper fin on the tail makes the shark swim in an upward direction all the time. This keeps the shark from sinking.

Strange though it seems, the shark sinks when it stops swimming. Most fish have air pockets inside their bodies that help them float, but sharks do not.

Here is a long tail with flat sides.
Does it move like the beaver tail?
Or does it move like the shark tail?
Can you tell how this tail is useful?

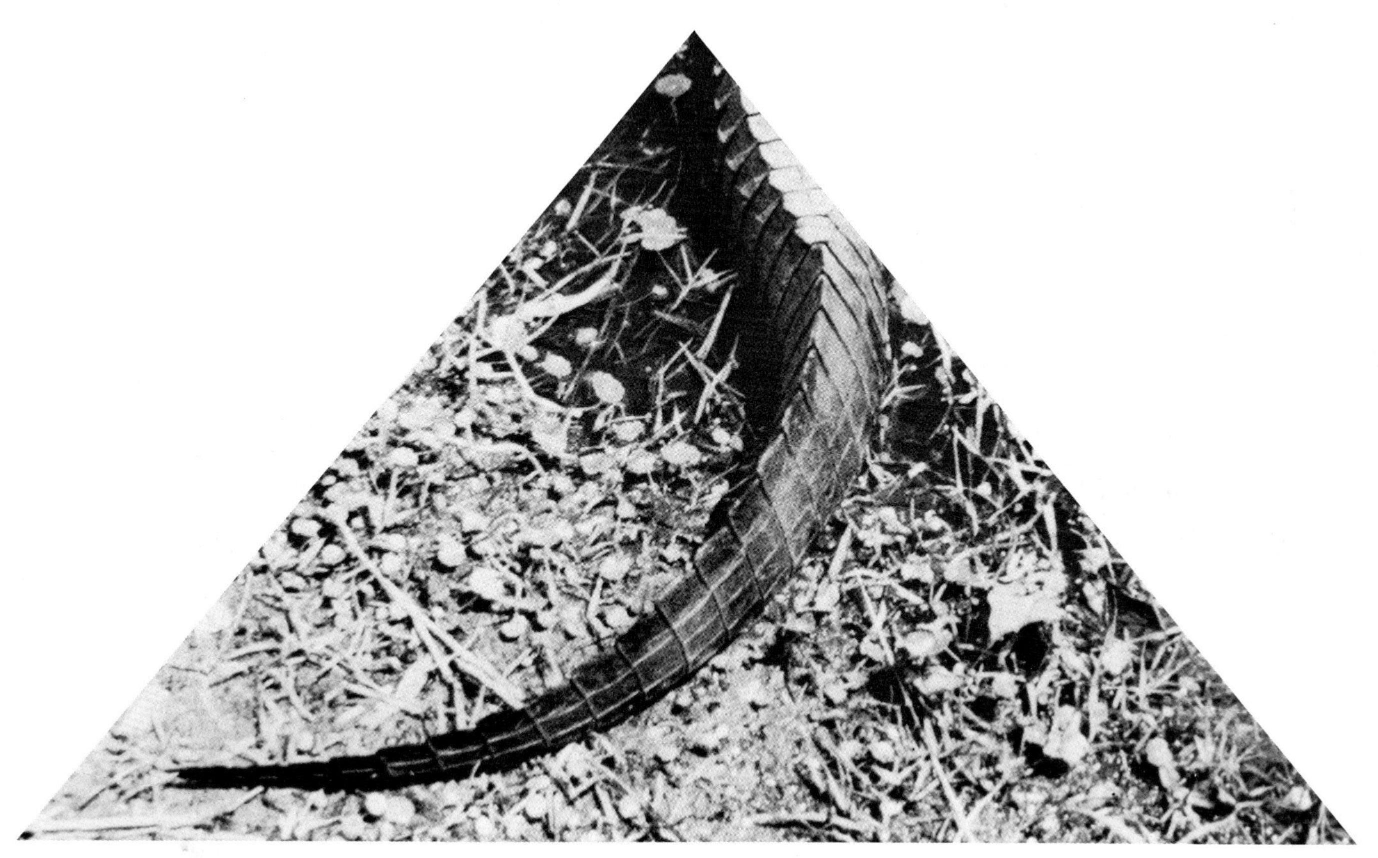

Like the shark, the **alligator** moves its tail from side to side. This is a tail with power. It can move the alligator silently and swiftly through the water.

Bird tails are different from tails you have seen so far. Most animal tails are an extension of the backbone. The tail is formed of bone, muscle, and skin.

The tail of a bird is, too, but you cannot see that on a live bird. What you see are tail feathers that grow out of the tail and cover it.

How are these tail feathers used?

The **hawk**, like most birds, uses its flat tail feathers to steer its way through the air. By tipping them from side to side, a bird can change direction quickly. That is what a hawk needs to do when it is chasing a mouse for dinner.

By shifting their tail feathers,
birds can change the shape of their tails
to serve different needs.
These birds are **mallard ducks.**
When they tip tail-up to search for food
along the bottom of a river, they fold their
tail feathers into a streamlined point.

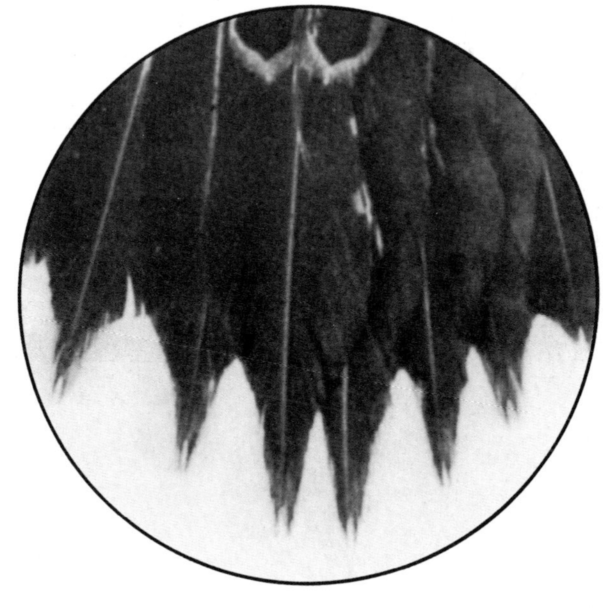

Here are tail feathers that are stiff as spikes. How are they useful to this bird?

A **flicker** has a special use for its flat tail. It holds the bird in place when hopping up a tree trunk.

Each tail feather is sharp as a dart and digs into the tree. With such a brace, the bird can safely move up or down or sideways.

When flying, the flicker uses its tail to steer and brake, just like other birds do.

Have you ever looked behind a peacock's fancy tail?
Those short, dull brown feathers are the true tail.
Their job is to support the long, colorful show-off feathers.

The **peacock's** fan-shaped tail is for show. Show-off feathers send the message, "Look at me. I am the best. Choose me."

Show-off tails mostly belong to male birds who use them to attract a mate.

This is a show-off tail found on both males and females.
The birds swing their tails so that the tips flutter
like leaves in a wind.
Why do you suppose they do that?

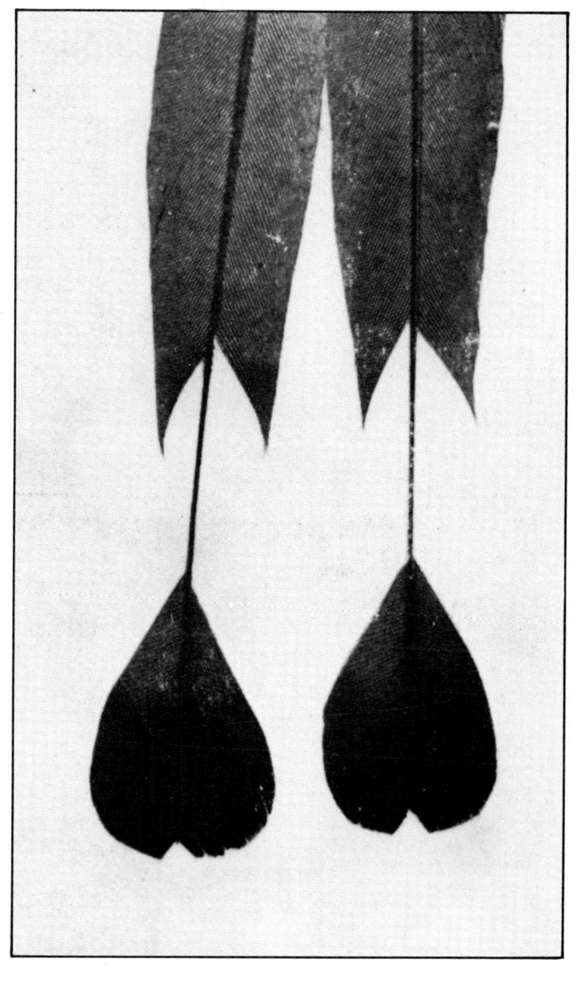

Mexican **mot-mots** are brightly colored, but it is still hard to see them in the tropical forests where they live. There are too many leaves and colorful flowers.

To let other mot-mots know where they are they flutter their tails. The tips of the two middle feathers swing wildly because they have been picked bare just above the ends.

Mot-mots are the only birds known to change the shape of their own tails.

What animal has a tail when it is young,
but not when it is grown-up?

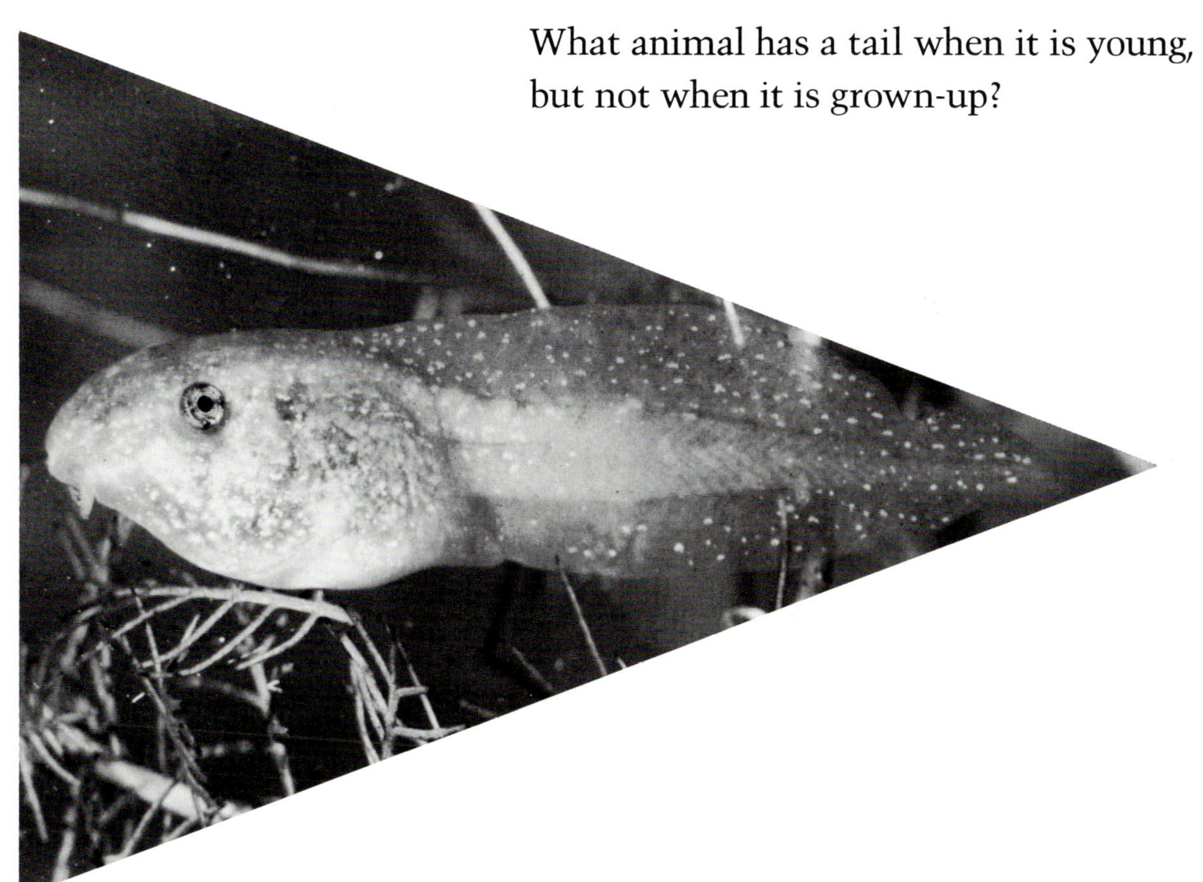

A **tadpole's** tail is useful for swimming.
This tadpole is shown much larger than life size.
Two-thirds of it is tail.

When a tadpole becomes a frog, the tail disappears. A **frog** has no need for a tail.

The frog lives on land as much as in the water. On land a frog uses its long legs to hop. In the water it uses its feet for swimming.

This is the tail of a desert animal. Its body is covered with a horny shell. When it swings its tail, it means business. Can you tell what that business is?

The **scorpion** uses its tail for defense. The tip has a stinger that contains poison.

Some scorpions have a poison strong enough to kill a human. The poison can also be used to paralyze animals the scorpion intends to eat.

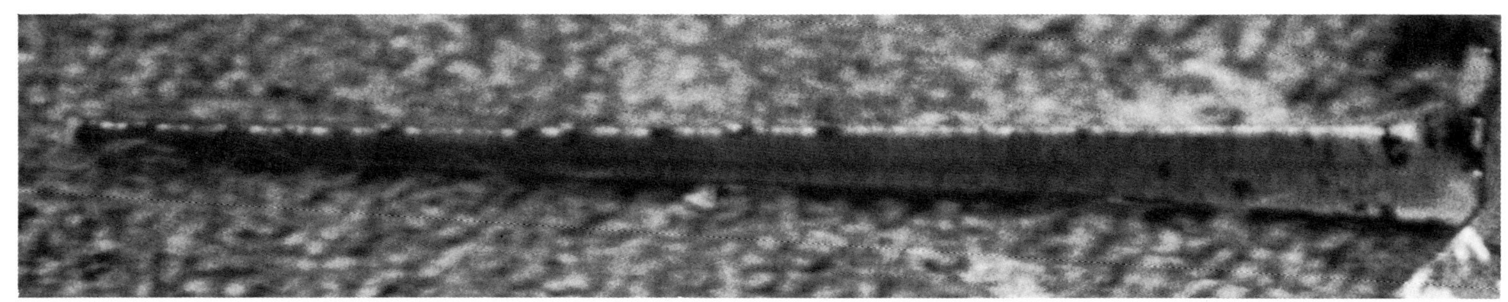

This tail is stiff and pointed.
It belongs to an animal that lives at the edge of the ocean. The tail cannot bend, but it can move in all directions.
If a wave threw this animal onto its back, how could its tail be useful?

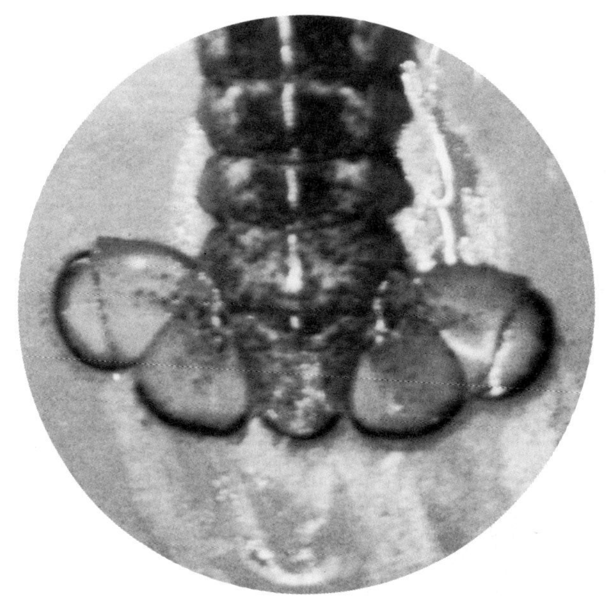

Here is a fan-shaped tail that works in the water.
It moves downward toward the body of the animal.
Can you tell what this tail does?

When a **horseshoe crab** is thrown on its back, it waves its legs helplessly—for a moment. Then it swivels its stiff tail around, jabs it into the sand and turns itself over.

When swimming, the tail acts like a rudder to steer the crab in one direction or another.

A **lobster** swims by shooting itself through the water. Each time the tail snaps downward toward the body, it moves the lobster with a jetlike burst of speed.

The tails of lobsters, horseshoe crabs, and scorpions belong to animals that do not have bones.

These animals have their soft parts inside their bodies and their hard parts—or skeletons—outside their bodies. Their tails are made of the same horny or shell-like materials that cover their bodies.

These tails are not very long and not very wide. They have tassels of black hair. When the animal whisks its tail back and forth, the tail does a good job.

What can that be?

Whether it is the tail of a **wild horse** or of a domestic horse, it makes a good flyswatter. The wild horses opposite are called onagers. They live in desert areas of the Middle East where there are many flies and biting insects to bother them.

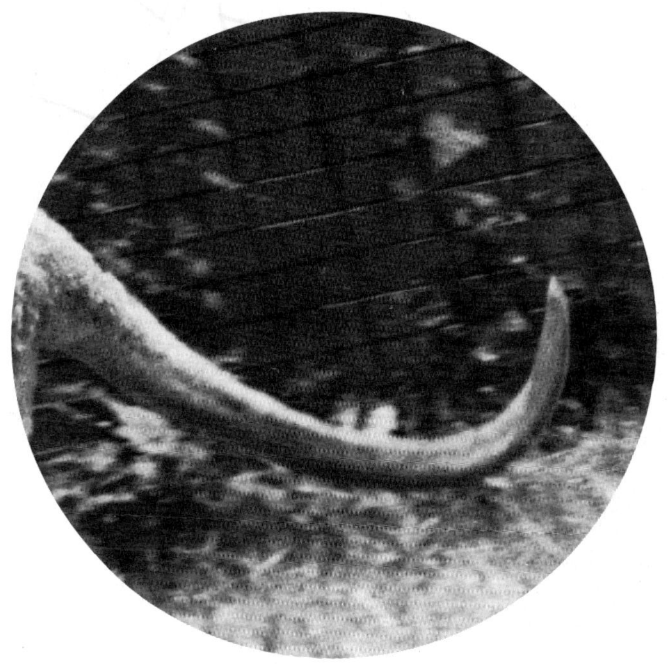

This tail is as long as the animal's body. The large, heavy tail is very useful. Do you know what it is used for?

When a **red kangaroo** leans forward to move fast, the weight of its tail balances the weight of its body. It can leap twenty or more feet and move at speeds of thirty miles an hour or more.

When leaping, the tail acts as a rudder, giving the animal the ability to turn quickly. When standing, fighting, or moving slowly, the kangaroo uses its tail as a brace.

Some lizards use their tails
in very strange ways.
Can you tell what has
happened to this tail?

Some lizards can drop off their tails when being chased. The attacking animal chases the still-wiggling tail while the lizard gets away.

This is how the **leopard gecko** looked before dropping its tail. On the previous page you can see the new tail beginning to grow.

Lizards are one of the few animals that can regrow lost parts.

Does this look like a tail?
The fat tail of this lizard
has a surprising use.
Can you tell what this is?

The tail of the **stump-tailed lizard** is a decoy.
The short-legged, fat lizard cannot move quickly
to escape an animal that would eat it.
With a tail that looks like a head,
the lizard can fool its enemy.
Because it is hard to tell which way the lizard is going,
the attacker may strike the tail instead of the head.
The stump-tailed lizard could live with a bite on the tail,
but would probably not live if bitten on the head.

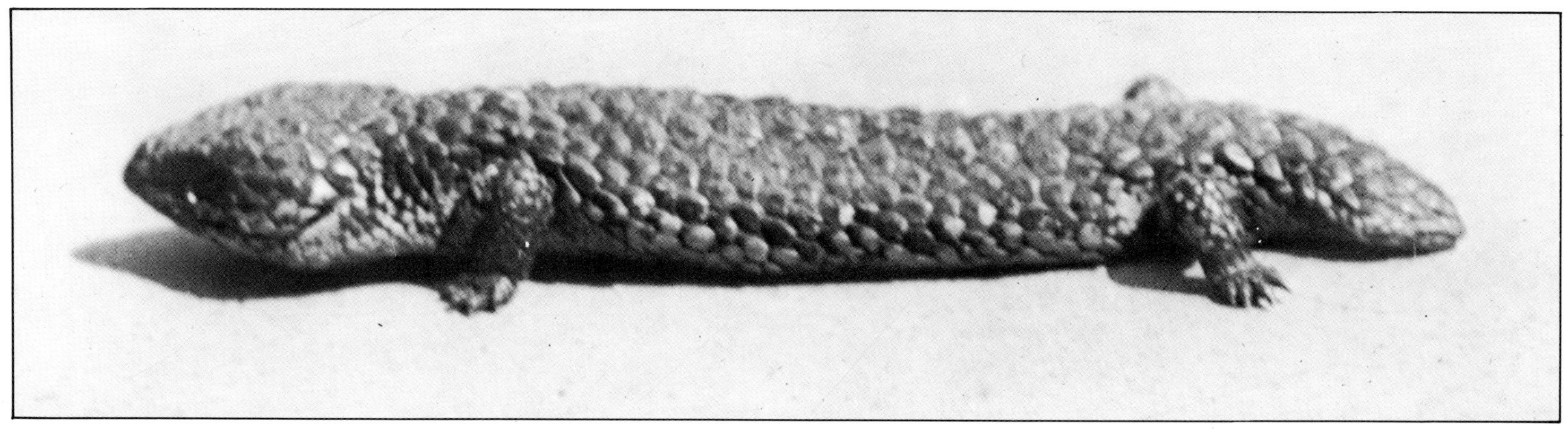

Here is a long tail on a very small animal.
The tail does not help the animal move.
It helps it to stop.
Do you know this tail?

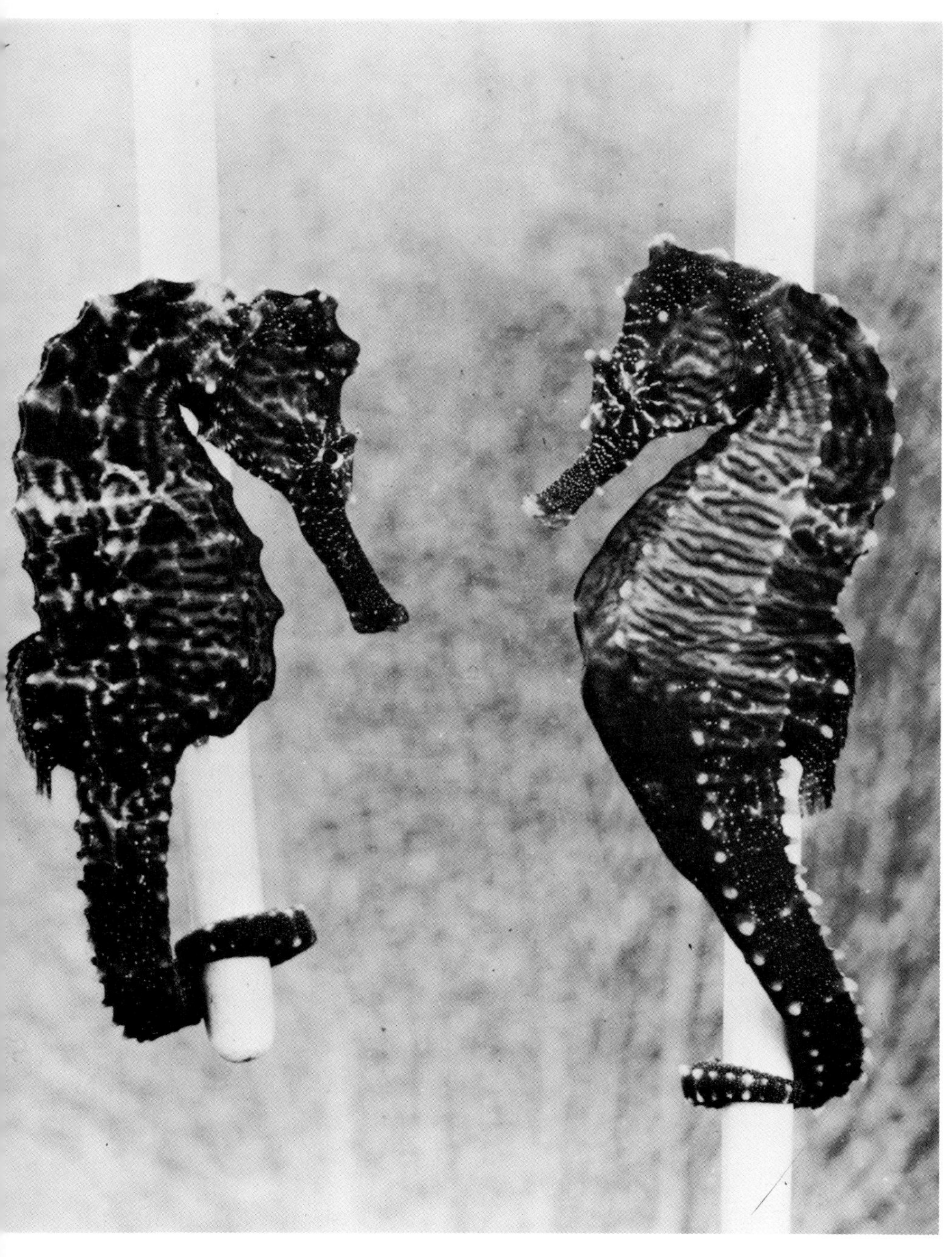

Sea horses hold onto seaweeds with their tails. When they let go, they float with the ocean currents.

The tails do not steer them or help them move, but they do help them stop moving.

A sea horse can reach out with its tail and grab almost anything it passes, from a stick to a piece of seaweed. That stops it from moving.

This tail is long and strong.
It does its job by curling around
a branch and holding tightly.
What good is a tail that curls
around a branch?

The **prehensile-tailed skink** has a tail to hang by. Its tail can hold its weight while it scrambles for a footing. A skink's short legs are not much good for climbing trees without the help of its tail. (Pre-hen-sile means able to grasp something.)

This is a long, hairy tail.
How is it like the tail of a skink?

The **spider monkey** has a prehensile tail, too. Its tail helps it climb trees in tropical forests in South America. With four long legs and a tail that can grasp branches, this monkey lives 180 feet above the ground. There it collects fruit and nuts that other animals cannot reach.

Tails can be very useful.
Would you like to have one?
If you could order the tail of your choice,
what kind of tail would you want?
And what would you want to do with it?

Index

Alligator, 17, 18, 47

Beaver, 8, 10
Bird tails
  duck, mallard, 21
  flicker, 21, 22
  hawk, 19, 20
  mot-mot, 25, 26
  peacock, 23, 24

Deer, white-tailed, 9, 11
Definition of a tail, 14, 19, 33
Duck, mallard, 21

Flicker, 21, 22
Frog, 28
  tadpole, 27

Hawk, 19, 20
Horseshoe crab, 31, 32

Kangaroo, 35, 36

Leopard gecko, 37, 38, 47
Lizard
  leopard gecko, 37, 38, 47
  prehensile-tailed skink, 43, 44
  stump-tailed, 39, 40
Lobster, 31, 33, 47

Monkey, spider, 45, 46
Mot-mot, 25, 26

Onager, 34, 35

Peacock, 23, 24

Scorpion, 29, 30
Sea horse, 41, 42
Shark, sand tiger, 15, 16
Skink, prehensile-tailed, 43, 44
Skunk, 5, 6, 7
Snake, 13
  rattlesnake, 9, 12
  skeleton, 14
Stump-tailed lizard, 39, 40

Tail shapes
  bumpy, 9, 12
  changing, 21, 26
  fan, 24, 31
  fat, 39
  flat, 8, 10, 15, 16, 17, 22
  fluffy, 5, 9
  long, 17, 23, 35, 41, 43, 45
  pointed, 21, 31
  short, 23, 34
  stiff, 21, 31, 32
  tasseled, 34

Tail uses
  balance, 36
  brace, 10, 22, 36
  brake, 22, 42
  decoy, 40
  defense, 30
  drop-off, 38
  flyswatter, 35
  prehensile, 44, 46
  propulsion, 16, 18, 27, 33
  show-off, 23, 24, 25
  signals and messages, 6, 7, 8, 10, 11, 12
  steer, 10, 16, 20, 22, 32, 36
Tails without backbones, 29, 31, 32, 33

Wild horses, 34, 35